SINGLE STRING STUDIES
For 6-String Bass Guitar

Volume One

By
Bruce Arnold

Muse Eek Publishing Company
New York, New York

Copyright © 2003 by Muse Eek Publishing Company. All rights reserved

ISBN-13: 978-1-890944-97-1

No part of this publication may be reproduced, stored in a
retrieval system, or transmitted, in any form or by any means,
electronic, mechanical, photocopying, recording, or otherwise,
without the prior written permission of the publisher.

Printed in the United States

This publication can be purchased from your local bookstore or by contacting:
Muse Eek Publishing Company
P.O. Box 509
New York, NY 10276, USA
866-415-8960-Toll Free In USA and Canada
Phone: 212-473-7030
Fax: 212-473-4601
http://www.muse-eek.com
sales@muse-eek.com

Table Of Contents

Acknowledgments	*v*
About the Author	*vi*
Foreword	*vii*
How to use this book	*viii*
Single String Exercise One: B string only	1
Single String Exercise Two: E string only	14
Single String Exercise Three: A string only	27
Single String Exercise Four: D string only	40
Single String Exercise Five: G string only	53
Single String Exercise Five: C string only (treble clef)	66
Single String Exercise Five: C string only (bass clef)	79
All Strings Exercise Six: all strings	92

Acknowledgments

The author would like to thank Oscar Rodriguez and Brian McBrearty for proof reading and helpful suggestions. I would also like to thank my students who through their questions helped me to see their needs so that I might address them as best I could.

About the Author

Born in Sioux Falls South Dakota, Bruce began his music training at the University of South Dakota. After three years of study he transferred to the Berklee College of Music where he received a Bachelor of Music degree in Composition. While doing undergraduate work at Berklee College of Music Bruce received the Harris Stanton award for outstanding guitarist of the year. He continued with further study in improvisational and compositional methods with Charlie Banacos and Jerry Bergonzi. Bruce received the outstanding teacher of the year award at Berklee in 1984 and went on to teach at the New England Conservatory of Music, and Dartmouth College.

Upon moving to New York City, Bruce found himself preoccupied with the possibilities of applying the twelve tone theoretical constructs of Schoenberg and Berg to American improvised music. His first CD, Blue Eleven contained the seeds of those ideas he was to develop further in his following critically acclaimed works: "A Few Dozen" and "Give 'Em Some." In this vein, his music is remarkably tonal, and the results give proof that inventive improvisation is possible within this format.

Bruce currently plays with his own band, "The Bruce Arnold Trio" and with "Spooky Actions" a jazz quartet that performs his transcriptions of Webern. In addition, Bruce has performed with such diverse musicians as Gary Burton, Joe Pass, Joe Lovano, Randy Brecker, Peter Erskine, Stuart Hamm, Boston Symphony Orchestra, and The Absolute Ensemble under the baton of Kristjan Järvi.

Bruce currently teaches at Princeton University, New York University and the New School. Upon his arrival at NYU he set about to improve the music education program, and instituted NYU's first sight-reading program for jazz guitarists. He started writing music education books to fill a need he perceived in formal jazz education.

As an author, Bruce has written 42 books on music education. These books cover many of the important aspects of mastering high performance skills for both the advanced music student with professional goals, and the dedicated beginner. To view the complete catalogue, please log on to his publisher's website at: http://www.muse-eek.com.

Foreword

Many of my students have asked me how they can improve their knowledge of the fretboard and recognition of notes on the bass. This book is an attempt to fill those needs.

Volume one of single string studies series aims at getting a student proficient at recognizing and playing notes on the bass. By limiting each exercise to one string it allows a student the chance to gain a familiarity with the notes found on each string. This in turn will also help a student to just "feel" where the notes are on each string rather than looking down at the instrument.

Each exercise is accompanied by an audio example. These audio examples can be downloaded for free from the internet at http://www.muse-eek.com. The audio files use midifiles which can be played on a Mac or IBM computer by using a midifileplayer or any sequencer program. Midifile players are available for free at many sites on the internet. muse-eek.com lists a few places to download this software.

See the final pages of this book for a complete listing and description of current music related publications.

Bruce Arnold
New York, New York

How to use this book

This book's purpose is to help a student learn the notes on each string of the 6-string bass guitar. There are some definite right and wrong ways to approach this goal. If you are a beginner at trying to read music on the bass guitar you will find it most challenging. Stringed instruments are unique in that there are so many places to play the same note. For example, the 6-string bass guitar has 5 places to play a B one half step below middle C (there is no B one half step below middle C found on the C string). Example One shows the location of middle C in the bass clef and a B one half step below middle C. Example Two shows the five places this note can be found.

Example One

Example Two: 5 positions of a B one half step below middle C on the 6-string bass.

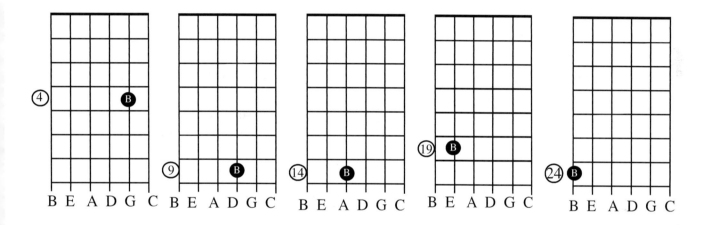

You can easily see that this can present a problem for a bassist. Just to play one note a decision has to be made on which string to use.

To further complicate things, the bass is a transposing instrument sounding one octave below the written note. Therefore if you see the note C one octave below middle C written on the staff you will play the C on the 3rd fret of the A string (see example Three).

Example Three

When you see this note in bass music

It will be played here on the 6-string bass

But the pitch you are actually hearing is:

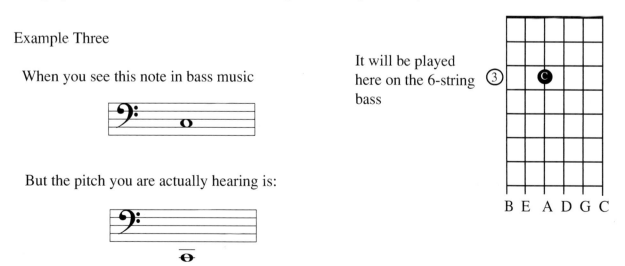

viii

You can see that you are sounding a pitch an octave below any written note when you read bass music. Many composers do not realize this so you will many times encounter a situation where you have to transpose your part up or down an octave. Just to recap a little, you have 5 actual pitches that correspond to the B one octave below middle C, (see example one) but because the bass is transposed down one octave you will be playing a sound that is one octave below the written pitch.

Students find this concept to be quite confusing. Therefore here is the example from the previous page explained one more time. If you are reading a part written for bass then it has been transposed. If you see a C one octave below middle C written, the pitch that will sound in reality is the C two ledger lines below the bass clef. (See example Four)

Example Four

If you play this written pitch

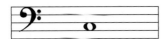

The bass will sound this pitch

All examples found in this book are written for the bass guitar and therefore have been transposed. If you see a middle C on the staff you will play this note at the fifth fret on the G string (See example Five) or at any of the other places you can find this note as previously discussed.

Example Five

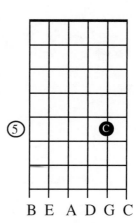

viii

The open strings on the 6-string bass guitar would be written as follows:

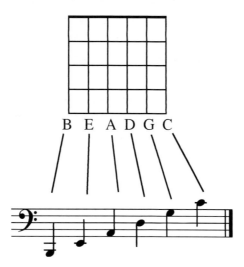

Keep in mind that with a 6 string bass you will often be required to read in the treble clef. So another way of portraying the open strings would be.

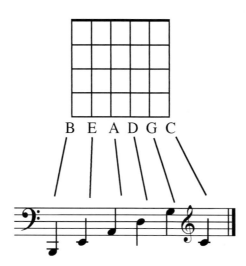

When you work on the examples found in this book do not look at your bass to find the pitch. One of the main ideas of this book is to get a student proficient at knowing where a note is by feel, not by looking at the fretboard. I recommend playing these exercises with a major chord drone for each key. For example if you are in C major, record a repeating C chord and use your ear to help you confirm if you are playing the right pitch.

These exercises should be played quite slow to begin with. When you reach Exercise 8 and begin playing notes on any string take advantage of open strings so you can keep your fretting hand above the 12th fret as much as possible. This will prepare you for the high ledger line notes that show up more often than you probably would like.

This book contains ledger lines up to 6 lines above the staff. It is uncommon to find the bass notated above the 3rd ledger line. If notes are needed above this range it is common to find them notated in the treble clef. With the advent of 5 and 6 string basses a bassist must prepare themselves for these higher ledger lines and also learn to read in the treble clef. Therefore it is suggested that you get a copy of the treble clef version of this book so you can get proficient at reading in the treble clef.

SINGLE STRING EXERCISE 1
BASS CLEF
B String Only
In C Major

1

SINGLE STRING EXERCISE 1
BASS CLEF
B String Only
In F Major

SINGLE STRING EXERCISE 1

BASS CLEF

B String Only

In Bb Major

SINGLE STRING EXERCISE 1

BASS CLEF

B String Only

In Eb Major

SINGLE STRING EXERCISE 1

BASS CLEF
B String Only
In Ab Major

SINGLE STRING EXERCISE 1

BASS CLEF
B String Only
In Db Major

SINGLE STRING EXERCISE 1
BASS CLEF
B String Only
In Gb Major

SINGLE STRING EXERCISE 1

BASS CLEF

B String Only

In F# Major

SINGLE STRING EXERCISE 1
BASS CLEF
B String Only
In B Major

SINGLE STRING EXERCISE 1
BASS CLEF
B String Only
In E Major

SINGLE STRING EXERCISE 1

BASS CLEF
B String Only
In A Major

SINGLE STRING EXERCISE 1

BASS CLEF
B String Only
In D Major

SINGLE STRING EXERCISE 1

BASS CLEF

B String Only

In G Major

SINGLE STRING EXERCISE 2
BASS CLEF
E String Only

In C Major

SINGLE STRING EXERCISE 2

BASS CLEF
E String Only
In F Major

SINGLE STRING EXERCISE 2
BASS CLEF
E String Only

In Bb Major

SINGLE STRING EXERCISE 2

BASS CLEF
E String Only
In Eb Major

SINGLE STRING EXERCISE 2

BASS CLEF
E String Only
In Ab Major

SINGLE STRING EXERCISE 2

BASS CLEF
E String Only
In Db Major

SINGLE STRING EXERCISE 2
BASS CLEF
Low E String Only

Key Of Gb Major

SINGLE STRING EXERCISE 2

BASS CLEF

E String Only

In F# Major

SINGLE STRING EXERCISE 2
BASS CLEF
E String Only

In B Major

SINGLE STRING EXERCISE 2

BASS CLEF

E String Only

In E Major

SINGLE STRING EXERCISE 2
BASS CLEF
E String Only

In A Major

SINGLE STRING EXERCISE 2

BASS CLEF
E String Only
In D Major

SINGLE STRING EXERCISE 2

BASS CLEF

E String Only

In G Major

SINGLE STRING EXERCISE 3

BASS CLEF
A String Only

In C Major

SINGLE STRING EXERCISE 3
BASS CLEF
A String Only

In F Major

SINGLE STRING EXERCISE 3

BASS CLEF

A String Only

In Bb Major

SIGHT READING EXERCISE 3

BASS CLEF

A String Only

In Eb Major

SINGLE STRING EXERCISE 3
BASS CLEF
A String Only

In Ab Major

31

SINGLE STRING EXERCISE 3

BASS CLEF

A String Only

In Db Major

SINGLE STRING EXERCISE 3
BASS CLEF
A String Only

In Gb Major

SINGLE STRING EXERCISE 3

BASS CLEF

A String Only

In F# Major

SINGLE STRING EXERCISE 3

BASS CLEF

A String Only

In B Major

SINGLE STRING EXERCISE 3
BASS CLEF
A String Only
In E Major

SINGLE STRING EXERCISE 3

BASS CLEF

A String Only

In A Major

SINGLE STRING EXERCISE 3
BASS CLEF
A String Only
In D Major

SINGLE STRING EXERCISE 3
BASS CLEF
A String Only

In G Major

SINGLE STRING EXERCISE 4
BASS CLEF
D String Only
In C Major

SINGLE STRING EXERCISE 4

BASS CLEF
D String Only
In F Major

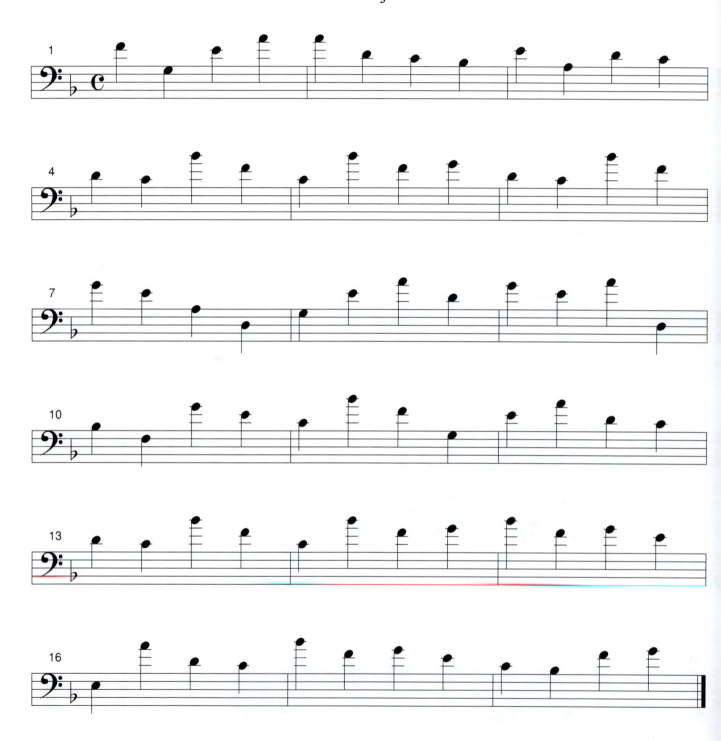

SINGLE STRING EXERCISE 4
BASS CLEF
D String Only
In Bb Major

SINGLE STRING EXERCISE 4

BASS CLEF

D String Only

In Eb Major

43

SINGLE STRING EXERCISE 4

BASS CLEF
D String Only
In Ab Major

SINGLE STRING EXERCISE 4

BASS CLEF

D String Only

In Db Major

SINGLE STRING EXERCISE 4
BASS CLEF
D String Only

In Gb Major

SINGLE STRING EXERCISE 4
BASS CLEF
D String Only
In F# Major

SINGLE STRING EXERCISE 4
BASS CLEF
D String Only
In B Major

SINGLE STRING EXERCISE 4
BASS CLEF
D String Only
In E Major

SINGLE STRING EXERCISE 4
BASS CLEF
D String Only
In A Major

SINGLE STRING EXERCISE 4
BASS CLEF
D String Only
In D Major

SINGLE STRING EXERCISE 4

BASS CLEF

D String Only

In G Major

SINGLE STRING EXERCISE 5
BASS CLEF
G String Only
In C Major

SINGLE STRING EXERCISE 5
BASS CLEF
G String Only
In F Major

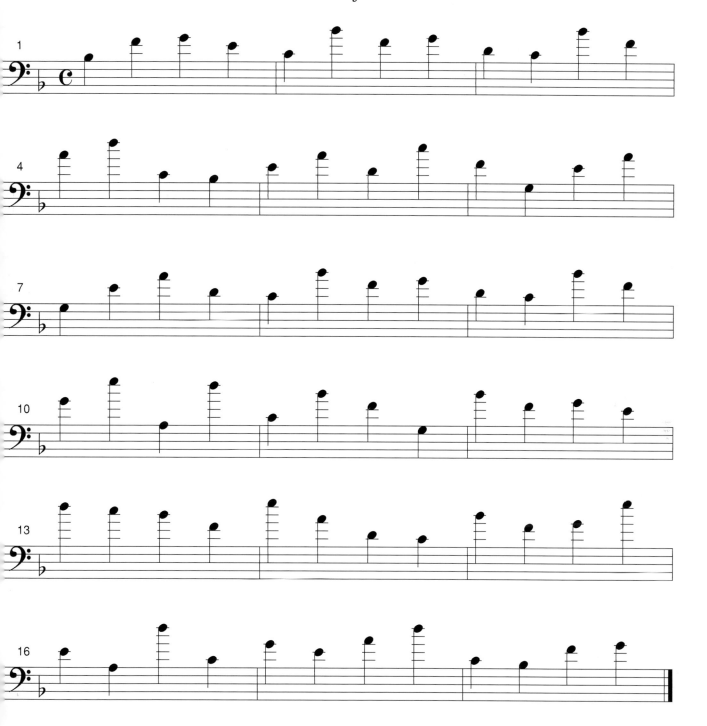

SINGLE STRING EXERCISE 5
BASS CLEF
G String Only
In Bb Major

SINGLE STRING EXERCISE 5

BASS CLEF
G String Only
In Eb Major

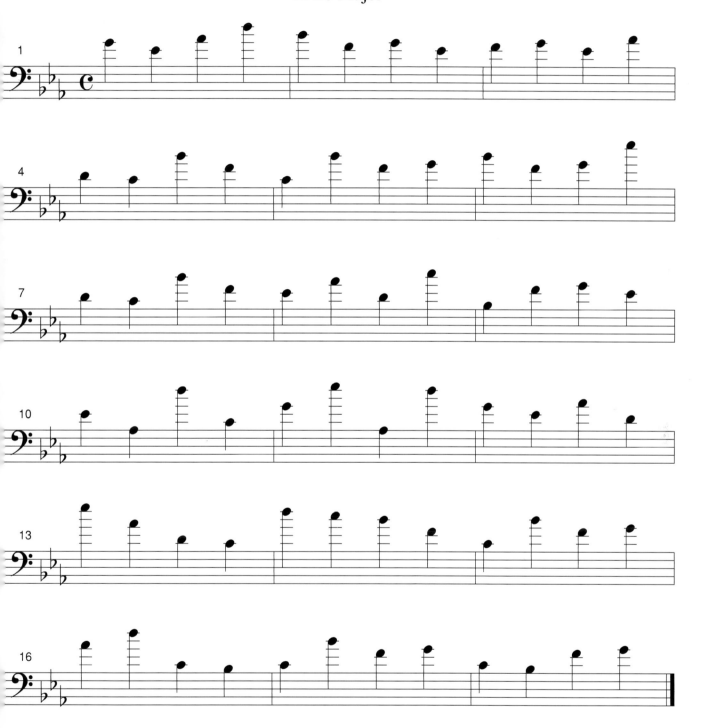

SINGLE STRING EXERCISE 5
BASS CLEF
G String Only
In Ab Major

SINGLE STRING EXERCISE 5
BASS CLEF
G String Only
In Db Major

SINGLE STRING EXERCISE 5
BASS CLEF
G String Only
In Gb Major

SINGLE STRING EXERCISE 5
BASS CLEF
G String Only
In F# Major

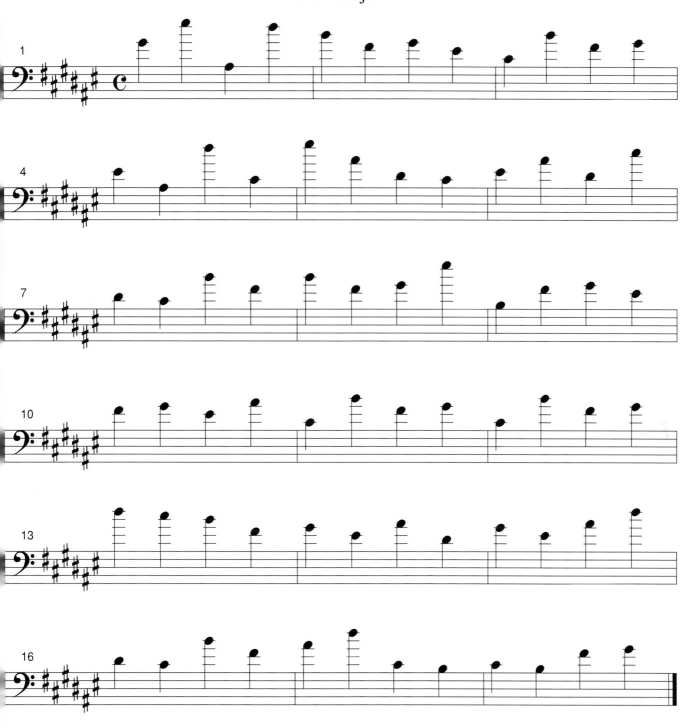

SINGLE STRING EXERCISE 5

BASS CLEF
G String Only
In B Major

SINGLE STRING EXERCISE 5

BASS CLEF
G String Only
In E Major

SINGLE STRING EXERCISE 5

BASS CLEF

G String Only

In A Major

SINGLE STRING EXERCISE 5
BASS CLEF
G String Only

In D Major

SINGLE STRING EXERCISE 5
BASS CLEF
G String Only
In G Major

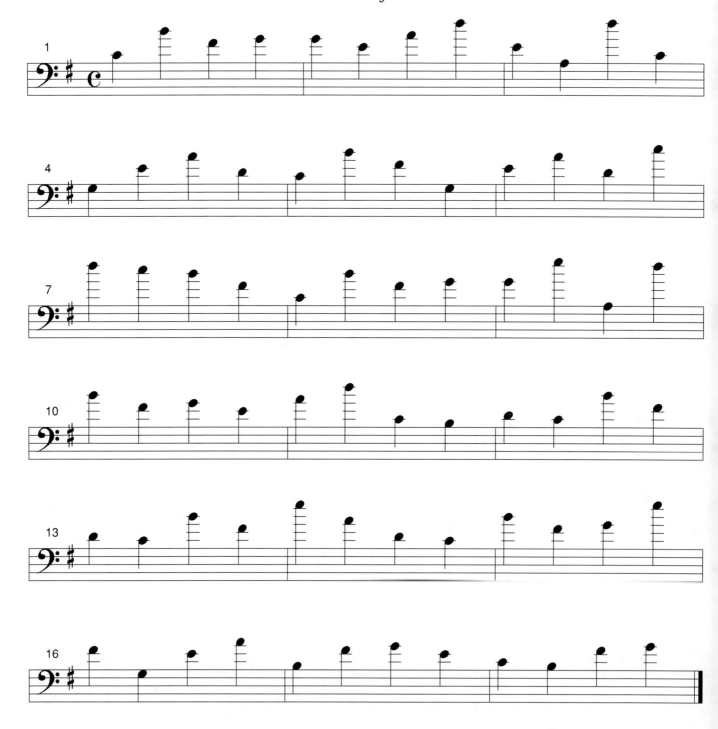

SINGLE STRING EXERCISE 6
TREBLE CLEF
C String Only

In C Major

SINGLE STRING EXERCISE 6
TREBLE CLEF

C String Only

In F Major

SINGLE STRING EXERCISE 6
TREBLE CLEF
C String Only
In Bb Major

SINGLE STRING EXERCISE 6
TREBLE CLEF
C String Only
In Eb Major

SINGLE STRING EXERCISE 6
TREBLE CLEF
C String Only
In Ab Major

SINGLE STRING EXERCISE 6
TREBLE CLEF
C String Only
In Db Major

SINGLE STRING EXERCISE 6
TREBLE CLEF

C String Only

In Gb Major

SINGLE STRING EXERCISE 6
TREBLE CLEF

C String Only

In F# Major

SINGLE STRING EXERCISE 6
TREBLE CLEF
C String Only
In B Major

SINGLE STRING EXERCISE 6
TREBLE CLEF

C String Only

In E Major

SINGLE STRING EXERCISE 6
TREBLE CLEF
C String Only
In A Major

SINGLE STRING EXERCISE 6
TREBLE CLEF
C String Only
In D Major

SINGLE STRING EXERCISE 6
TREBLE CLEF
C String Only

In G Major

SINGLE STRING EXERCISE 7
BASS CLEF
C String Only
In C Major

SINGLE STRING EXERCISE 7
BASS CLEF
C String Only
In F Major

SINGLE STRING EXERCISE 7
BASS CLEF

C String Only

In Bb Major

SINGLE STRING EXERCISE 7

BASS CLEF

C String Only

In Eb Major

SINGLE STRING EXERCISE 7
BASS CLEF
C String Only
In Ab Major

SINGLE STRING EXERCISE 7
BASS CLEF
C String Only
In Db Major

SINGLE STRING EXERCISE 7
BASS CLEF
C String Only
In Gb Major

SINGLE STRING EXERCISE 7
BASS CLEF
C String Only
In F# Major

SINGLE STRING EXERCISE 7
BASS CLEF
C String Only
In B Major

SINGLE STRING EXERCISE 7
BASS CLEF
C String Only
In E Major

SINGLE STRING EXERCISE 7
BASS CLEF
C String Only
In A Major

SINGLE STRING EXERCISE 7
BASS CLEF
C String Only
In D Major

SINGLE STRING EXERCISE 7
BASS CLEF
C String Only
In G Major

ALL STRINGS EXERCISE 8
BASS and TREBLE CLEF
In C Major

ALL STRINGS EXERCISE 8
BASS and TREBLE CLEF
In F Major

ALL STRINGS EXERCISE 8
BASS and TREBLE CLEF
In Bb Major

ALL STRINGS EXERCISE 8
BASS and TREBLE CLEF
In Eb Major

ALL STRINGS EXERCISE 8
BASS and TREBLE CLEF
In Ab Major

ALL STRINGS EXERCISE 8
BASS and TREBLE CLEF
In Db Major

ALL STRINGS EXERCISE 8
BASS and TREBLE CLEF
In Gb Major

ALL STRINGS EXERCISE 8
BASS and TREBLE CLEF
In F# Major

ALL STRINGS EXERCISE 8
BASS and TREBLE CLEF
In B Major

ALL STRINGS EXERCISE 8
BASS and TREBLE CLEF
In E Major

ALL STRINGS EXERCISE 8
BASS and TREBLE CLEF
In A Major

ALL STRINGS EXERCISE 8
BASS and TREBLE CLEF
In D Major

ALL STRINGS EXERCISE 8
BASS and TREBLE CLEF
In G Major

Books Available From
Muse Eek Publishing Company

The Bruce Arnold series of instruction books for guitar are the result of 20 years of teaching. Mr. Arnold, who teaches at New York University and Princeton University has listened to the questions and problems of his students, and written forty books addressing the needs of the beginning to advanced student. Written in a direct, friendly and practical manner, each book is structured in such as way as to enable a student to understand, retain and apply musical information. In short, these books teach.

1st Steps for a Beginning Guitarist
Spiral Bound ISBN 1890944-90-4   Perfect Bound ISBN 1890944-93-9

"1st Steps for a Beginning Guitarist" is a comprehensive method for guitar students who have no prior musical training. Whether you are playing acoustic, electric or twelve-string guitar, this book will give you the information you need, and trouble shoot the various pitfalls that can hinder the self-taught musician. Includes pictures, videos and audio in the form of midifiles and mp3's.

Chord Workbook for Guitar Volume 1 (2nd edition)
Spiral Bound ISBN 0-9648632-1-9   Perfect Bound ISBN 1890944-50-5

A consistent seller, this book addresses the needs of the beginning through intermediate student. The beginning student will learn chords on the guitar, and a section is also included to help learn the basics of music theory. Progressions are provided to help the student apply these chords to common sequences. The more advanced student will find the reharmonization section to be an invaluable resource of harmonic choices. Information is given through musical notation as well as tablature.

Chord Workbook for Guitar Volume 2 (2nd edition)
Spiral Bound ISBN 0-9648632-3-5   Perfect Bound ISBN 1890944-51-3

This book is the Rosetta Stone of pop/jazz chords, and is geared to the intermediate to advanced student. These are the chords that any serious student bent on a musical career must know. Unlike other books which simply give examples of isolated chords, this unique book provides a comprehensive series of progressions and chord combinations which are immediately applicable to both composition and performance.

Music Theory Workbook for Guitar Series

The world's most popular instrument, the guitar, is not taught in our public schools. In addition, it is one of the hardest on which to learn the basics of music. As a result, it is frequently difficult for the serious guitarist to get a firm foundation in theory.

Theory Workbook for Guitar Volume 1
Spiral Bound ISBN 0-9648632-4-3   Perfect Bound ISBN 1890944-52-1

This book provides real hands-on application of intervals and chords. A theory section written in concise and easy to understand language prepares the student for all exercises. Worksheets are given that quiz a student about intervals and chord construction using staff notation and guitar tablature. Answers are supplied in the back of the book enabling a student to work without a teacher.

Theory Workbook for Guitar Volume 2
Spiral Bound ISBN 0-9648632-5-1   Perfect Bound ISBN 1890944-53-X

This book provides real hands-on application for 22 different scale types. A theory section written in concise and easy to understand language prepares the student for all exercises. Worksheets are given that quiz a student about scale construction using staff notation and guitar tablature. Answers are supplied in the back of the book enabling a student to work without a teacher. Audio files are also available on the muse-eek.com website to facilitate practice and improvisation with all the scales presented.

Rhythm Book Series

These books are a breakthrough in music instruction, using the internet as a teaching tool! Audio files of all the exercises are easily downloaded from the internet.

Rhythm Primer
Spiral Bound ISBN 0-890944-03-3   Perfect Bound ISBN 1890944-59-9

This 61 page book concentrates on all basic rhythms using four rhythmic levels. All examples use one pitch, allowing the student to focus completely on time and rhythm. All exercises can be downloaded from the internet to facilitate learning. See http://www.muse-eek.com for details

Rhythms Volume 1
Spiral Bound ISBN 0-9648632-7-8   Perfect Bound ISBN 1890944-55-6

This 120 page book concentrates on eighth note rhythms and is a thesaurus of rhythmic patterns. All examples use one pitch, allowing the student to focus completely on time and rhythm. All exercises can be downloaded from the internet to facilitate learning. See http://www.muse-eek.com for details.

Rhythms Volume 2
Spiral Bound ISBN 0-9648632-8-6   Perfect Bound ISBN 1890944-56-4

This volume concentrates on sixteenth note rhythms, and is a 108 page thesaurus of rhythmic patterns. All examples use one pitch, allowing the student to focus completely on time and rhythm. All exercises can be downloaded from the internet to facilitate learning. See http://www.muse-eek.com for details.

Rhythms Volume 3
Spiral Bound ISBN 0-890944-04-1   Perfect Bound ISBN 1890944-57-2

This volume concentrates on thirty second note rhythms, and is a 102 page thesaurus of rhythmic patterns. All examples use one pitch, allowing the student to focus completely on time and rhythm. All exercises can be downloaded from the internet to facilitate learning. See http://www.muse-eek.com for details.

Odd Meters Volume 1
Spiral Bound ISBN 0-9648632-9-4   Perfect Bound ISBN 1890944-58-0

This book applies both eighth and sixteenth note rhythms to odd meter combinations. All examples use one pitch, allowing the student to focus completely on time and rhythm. Exercises can be downloaded from the internet to facilitate learning. This 100 page book is an essential sight reading tool. See http://www.muse-eek.com for details.

Contemporary Rhythms Volume 1
Spiral Bound ISBN 1-890944-27-0   Perfect Bound ISBN 1890944-84-X

This volume concentrates on eight note rhythms and is a thesaurus of rhythmic patterns. Each exercise uses one pitch which allows the student to focus completely on time and rhythm. Exercises use modern innovations common to twentieth century notation, thereby familiarizing the student with the most sophisticated systems likely to be encountered in the course of a musical career. All exercises can be downloaded from the internet to facilitate learning. See http://www.muse-eek.com for details.

Contemporary Rhythms Volume 2
Spiral Bound ISBN 1-890944-28-9   Perfect Bound ISBN 1890944-85-8

This volume concentrates on sixteenth note rhythms and is a thesaurus of rhythmic patterns. Each exercise uses one pitch which allows the student to focus completely on time and rhythm. Exercise use modern innovations common to twentieth century notation, thereby familiarizing the student with the most sophisticated systems likely to be encountered in the course of a musical career. All exercises can be downloaded from the internet to facilitate learning. See http://www.muse-eek.com for details.

Independence Volume 1
Spiral Bound ISBN 1-890944-00-9   Perfect Bound ISBN 1890944-83-1

This 51 page book is designed for pianists, stick and touchstyle guitarists, percussionists and anyone who wishes to develop the rhythmic independence of their hands. This volume concentrates on quarter, eighth and sixteenth note rhythms and is a thesaurus of rhythmic patterns. The exercises in this book gradually incorporate more and more complex rhythmic patterns making it an excellent tool for both the beginning and the advanced   student.

Other Guitar Study Aids

Right Hand Technique for Guitar Volume 1
Spiral Bound ISBN 0-9648632-6-X   Perfect Bound ISBN 1890944-54-8

Here's a breakthrough in music instruction, using the internet as a teaching tool! This book gives a concise method for developing right hand technique on the guitar, one of the most overlooked and under-addressed aspects of learning the instrument. The simplest, most basic movements are used to build fatigue-free technique. Exercises can be downloaded from the internet to facilitate learning. See http://www.muse-eek.com for details.

Single String Studies Volume One
Spiral Bound ISBN 1-890944-01-7   Perfect Bound ISBN 1890944-62-9

This book is an excellent learning tool for both the beginner who has no experience reading music on the guitar, and the advanced student looking to improve their ledger line reading and general knowledge of each string of the guitar. Each exercise concentrates the students attention on one string at a time. This allows a familiarity to form between the written pitch and where it can be found on the guitar along with improving one's "feel" for jumping linearly across the fretboard. Exercises can be downloaded from the internet to facilitate learning. See http://www.muse-eek.com for details.

Single String Studies Volume Two
Spiral Bound ISBN 1-890944-05-X   Perfect Bound ISBN 1890944-64-5

This book is a continuation of Volume One, but using non-diatonic notes. Volume Two helps the intermediate and advanced student improve their ledger line reading and general knowledge of each string of the guitar. Each exercise concentrates the students attention on one string at a time. This allows a familiarity to form between the written pitch and where it can be found on the guitar along with improving one's "feel" for jumping linearly across the fretboard. Exercises can be downloaded from the internet to facilitate learning. See http://www.muse-eek.com for details.

Single String Studies Volume One (Bass Clef)
Spiral Bound ISBN 1-890944-02-5   Perfect Bound ISBN 1890944-63-7

This book is an excellent learning tool for both the beginner who has no experience reading music on the bass guitar, and the advanced student looking to improve their ledger line reading and general knowledge of each string of the bass. Each exercise concentrates a students attention of one string at a time. This allows a familiarity to form between the written pitch and where it can be found on the bass along with improving one's "feel" for jumping linearly across the fretboard. Exercises can be downloaded from the internet to facilitate learning. See http://www.muse-eek.com for details.

Single String Studies Volume Two (Bass Clef)
Spiral Bound ISBN 1-890944-06-8   Perfect Bound ISBN 1890944-65-3

This book is a continuation of Volume One, but using non-diatonic notes. Volume Two helps the intermediate and advanced student improve their ledger line reading and general knowledge of each string of the bass. Each exercise concentrates the students attention on one string at a time. This allows a familiarity to form between the written pitch and where it can be found on the bass along with improving one's "feel" for jumping linearly across the fretboard. Exercises can be downloaded from the internet to facilitate learning. See http://www.muse-eek.com for details.

Guitar Clinic
Spiral Bound ISBN 1-890944-45-9   Perfect Bound ISBN 1890944-86-6

Guitar Clinic" contains techniques and exercises Mr. Arnold uses in the clinics and workshops he teaches around the U.S.. Much of the material in this book is culled from Mr. Arnold's educational series, over thirty books in all. The student wishing to expand on his or her studies will find suggestions within the text as to which of Mr. Arnold's books will best serve their specific needs. Topics covered include: how to read music, sight reading, reading rhythms, music theory, chord and scale construction, modal sequencing, approach notes, reharmonization, bass and chord comping, and hexatonic scales.

The Essentials: Chord Charts, Scales, and Lead Patterns for the Guitar
Saddle Stitched (Stapled) ISBN 1-890944-94-7

This book is truly essential to the aspiring guitarist. It includes the most commonly played chords on the guitar in all keys, plus a bonus of the most commonly used scales and lead patterns. You can quickly learn all the chords, scales and lead patterns you need to know to play your favorite songs-and solo over them, too! "The Essentials" doesn't stop there, though. It also includes chord progressions to help you learn how to chord songs in folk, country, rock, blues and other popular styles. The books contain loads of easy to understand diagrams of chords, scales and lead patterns so you will be up and running in no time!

Sight Singing and Ear Training Series

The world is full of ear training and sight reading books, so why do we need more?
This sight singing and ear training series uses a different method of teaching relative pitch sight singing and ear training. The success of this method has been remarkable. Along with a new method of ear training these books also use CDs and the internet as a teaching tool! Audio files of all the exercises are easily downloaded from the internet at www.muse-eek.com By combining interactive audio files with a new approach to ear training a student's progress is limited only by their willingness to practice!

A Fanatic's Guide to Ear Training and Sight Singing
Spiral Bound ISBN 1-890944-19-X   Perfect Bound ISBN 1890944-75-0

This book and CD present a method for developing good pitch recognition through sight singing. This method differs from the myriad of other sight singing books in that it develops the ability to identify and name all twelve pitches within a key center. Through this method a student gains the ability to identify sound based on it's relationship to a key and not the relationship of one note to another (i.e. interval training as commonly taught in many texts). All note groupings from one to six notes are presented giving the student a thesaurus of basic note combinations which develops sight singing and note recognition to a level unattainable before this Guide's existence.

Key Note Recognition
Spiral Bound ISBN 1-890944-30-3   Perfect Bound ISBN 1890944-77-7

This book and CD present a method for developing the ability to recognize the function of any note against a key. This method is a must for anyone who wishes to sound one note on an instrument or voice and instantly know what key a song is in. Through this method a student gains the ability to identify a sound based on its relationship to a key and not the relationship of one note to another (i.e. interval training as commonly taught in many texts). Key Center Recognition is a definite requirement before proceeding to two note ear training.

LINES Volume One: Sight Reading and Sight Singing Exercises
Spiral Bound ISBN 1-890944-09-2   Perfect Bound ISBN 1890944-76-9

This book can be used for many applications. It is an excellent source for easy half note melodies that a beginner can use to learn how to read music or for sight singing slightly chromatic lines. An intermediate or advanced student will find exercises for multi-voice reading. These exercises can also be used for multi-voice ear training. The book has the added benefit in that all exercises can be heard by downloading the audio files for each example. See http://www.muse-eek.com for details.

Ear Training ONE NOTE: Beginning Level
Spiral Bound ISBN 1-890944-12-2   Perfect Bound ISBN 1890944-66-1

This Book and Audio CD presents a new and exciting method for developing relative pitch ear training. It has been used with great success and is now finally available on CD. There are three levels available depending on the student's ability. This beginning level is recommended for students who have little or no music training.

Ear Training ONE NOTE: Intermediate Level
Spiral Bound ISBN 1-890944-13-0   Perfect Bound ISBN 1890944-67-X

This Audio CD and booklet presents a new and exciting method of developing relative pitch ear training. It has been used with great success and is now finally available on CD. This intermediate level is recommended for students who have had some music training but still find their skills need more development.

Ear Training ONE NOTE: Advanced Level
Spiral Bound ISBN 1-890944-14-9   Perfect Bound ISBN 1890944-68-8

This Audio CD and booklet presents a new and exciting method of developing relative pitch ear training. It has been used with great success and is now finally available on CD. There are three levels available depending on the student's ability. This advanced level is recommended for students who have worked with the intermediate level and now wish to perfect their skills.

Ear Training TWO NOTE: Beginning Level Volume One
Spiral Bound ISBN 1-890944-31-9   Perfect Bound ISBN 1890944-69-6

This Book and Audio CD continues the method of developing relative pitch ear training as set forth in the "Ear Training, One Note" series. There are six volumes in the beginning level series. Through practice, the student eventually gains the ability to recognize the key and the names of any two notes played simultaneously. Volume One concentrates on 5ths. Prerequisite: a strong grasp of the One Note method.

Ear Training TWO NOTE: Beginning Level Volume Two
Spiral Bound ISBN 1-890944-32-7   Perfect Bound ISBN 1890944-70-X

This Book and Audio CD continues the method of developing relative pitch ear training as set forth in the "Ear Training, One Note" series. There are six volumes in the beginning level series. Through practice, the student eventually gains the ability to recognize the key and the names of any two notes played simultaneously. Volume Two concentrates on 3rds. Prerequisite: a strong grasp of the One Note method.

Ear Training TWO NOTE: Beginning Level Volume Three
Spiral Bound ISBN 1-890944-33-5   Perfect Bound ISBN 1890944-71-8

This Book and Audio CD continues the method of developing relative pitch ear training as set forth in the "Ear Training, One Note" series. There are six volumes in the beginning level series. Through practice, the student eventually gains the ability to recognize the key and the names of any two notes played simultaneously. Volume Three concentrates on 6ths. Prerequisite: a strong grasp of the One Note method.

Ear Training TWO NOTE: Beginning Level Volume Four
Spiral Bound ISBN 1-890944-34-3   Perfect Bound ISBN 1890944-72-6

This Book and Audio CD continues the method of developing relative pitch ear training as set forth in the "Ear Training, One Note" series. There are six volumes in the beginning level series. Through practice, the student eventually gains the ability to recognize the key and the names of any two notes played simultaneously. Volume Four concentrates on 4ths. Prerequisite: a strong grasp of the One Note method.

Ear Training TWO NOTE: Beginning Level Volume Five
Spiral Bound ISBN 1-890944-35-1   Perfect Bound ISBN 1890944-73-4

This Book and Audio CD continues the method of developing relative pitch ear training as set forth in the "Ear Training, One Note" series. There are six volumes in the beginning level series. Through practice, the student eventually gains the ability to recognize the key and the names of any two notes played simultaneously. Volume Five concentrates on 2nds. Prerequisite: a strong grasp of the One Note method.

Ear Training TWO NOTE: Beginning Level Volume Six
Spiral Bound ISBN 1-890944-36-X   Perfect Bound ISBN 1890944-74-2

This Book and Audio CD continues the method of developing relative pitch ear training as set forth in the "Ear Training, One Note" series. There are six volumes in the beginning level series. Through practice, the student eventually gains the ability to recognize the key and the names of any two notes played simultaneously. Volume Six concentrates on 7ths. Prerequisite: a strong grasp of the One Note method.

Comping Styles Series

This series is built on the progressions found in Chord Workbook Volume One. Each book covers a specific style of music and presents exercises to help a guitarist, bassist or drummer master that style. Audio CDs are also available so a student can play along with each example and really get "into the groove."

Comping Styles for the Guitar Volume Two FUNK
Spiral Bound ISBN 1-890944-07-6   Perfect Bound ISBN 1890944-60-2

This volume teaches a student how to play guitar or piano in a funk style. 36 Progressions are presented: 12 keys of a Major and Minor Blues plus 12 keys of Rhythm Changes A different groove is presented for each exercise giving the student a wide range of funk rhythms to master.   An Audio CD is also included so a student can play along with each example and really get "into the groove." The audio CD contains "trio" versions of each exercise with Guitar, Bass and Drums.

Comping Styles for the Bass Volume Two FUNK
Spiral Bound ISBN 1-890944-08-4   Perfect Bound ISBN 1890944-61-0

This volume teaches a student how to play bass in a funk style. 36 Progressions are presented: 12 keys of a Major and Minor Blues plus 12 keys of Rhythm Changes A different groove is presented for each exercise giving the student a wide range of funk rhythms to master.   An Audio CD is also included so a student can play along with each example and really get "into the groove." The audio CD contains "trio" versions of each exercise with Guitar, Bass and Drums.

Jazz and Blues Bass Line
Spiral Bound ISBN 1-890944-15-7   Perfect Bound ISBN 1890944-16-5

This book covers the basics of bass line construction. A theoretical guide to building bass lines is presented along with 36 chord progressions utilizing the twelve keys of a Major and Minor Blues, plus twelve keys of Rhythm Changes. A reharmonization section is also provided which demonstrates how to reharmonize a chord progression on the spot.

Time Series

The Doing Time series presents a method for contacting, developing and relying on your internal time sense: This series is an excellent source for any musician who is serious about developing strong internal sense of time. This is particularly useful in any kind of music where the rhythms and time signatures may be very complex or free, and there is no conductor.

THE BIG METRONOME
Spiral Bound ISBN   1-890944-37-8   Perfect Bound ISBN 1890944-82-3

The Big Metronome is designed to help you develop a better internal sense of time. This is accomplished by requiring you to "feel time" rather than having you rely on the steady click of a metronome. The idea is to slowly wean yourself away from an external device and rely on your internal/natural sense of time. The exercises presented work in conjunction with the three CDs that accompany this book. CD 1 presents the first 13 settings from a traditional metronome 40-66; the second CD contains metronome markings 69-116, and the third CD contains metronome markings 120-208. The first CD gives you a 2 bar count off and a click every measure, the second CD gives you a 2 bar count off and a click every 2 measures, the 3rd CD gives you a 2 bar count off and a click every 4 measures. By presenting all common metronome markings a student can use these 3 CDs as a replacement for a traditional metronome.

Doing Time with the Blues Volume One:
Spiral Bound ISBN 1-890944-17-3   Perfect Bound ISBN 1890944-78-5

The book and CD presents a method for gaining an internal sense of time thereby eliminating dependence on a metronome. The book presents the basic concept for developing good time and also includes exercises that can be practiced with the CD. The CD provides eight 8 minute tracks at different tempos in which the time is delineated every 2 bars, and with an extra hit every 12 bars to outline the blues form. The student may then use the exercises presented in the book to gain control of their execution or improvise to gain control of their ideas using this bare minimum of time delineation.

Doing Time with the Blues Volume Two:
Spiral Bound ISBN 1-890944-18-1   Perfect Bound ISBN 1890944-79-3

This is the 2nd volume of a four volume series which presents a method for developing a musician's internal sense of time, thereby eliminating dependence on a metronome. This 2nd volume presents different exercises which further the development of this time sense. This 2nd volume begins to test even a professional level player's ability. The CD provides eight 8 minute tracks at different tempos in which the time is delineated every 4 bars with an extra hit every 12 bars to outline the blues form. New exercises are also included that can be practiced with the CD. This series is an excellent source for any musician who is serious about developing an internal sense of time.

Doing Time with 32 bars Volume One:
Spiral Bound ISBN 1-890944-22-X   Perfect Bound ISBN Spiral Bound ISBN
1890944-80-7

The book and CD presents a method for gaining an internal sense of time thereby eliminating dependence on a metronome. The book presents the basic concept for developing good time and also includes exercises that can be practiced with the CD. The CD provides eight 8 minute tracks at different tempos in which the time is delineated every 2 bars, with an extra hit every 32 to outline the 32 bar form. The student may then use the exercises presented in the book to gain control of their execution or improvise to gain control of their ideas using this bare minimum of time delineation.

Doing Time with 32 bars Volume Two:
Spiral Bound ISBN 1-890944-23-8   Perfect Bound ISBN Spiral Bound ISBN
1890944-81-5

This is the 2nd volume of a four volume series which presents a method for developing a musician's internal sense of time, thereby eliminating dependence on a metronome.. This 2nd volume presents different exercises which further the development of this time sense. This 2nd volume begins to test even a professional level player's ability. The CD provides eight 8 minute tracks at different tempos in which the time is delineated every 4 bars with an extra hit every 32 bars to outline the 32 bar form.   New exercises are also included that can be practiced with the CD. This series is an excellent source for any musician who is serious about developing an internal sense of time.

Other Workbooks

Music Theory Workbook for All Instruments, Volume 1: Interval and Chord Construction
Spiral Bound ISBN 1890944-92-0   Perfect Bound ISBN 1890944-46-7

This book provides real hands-on application of intervals and chords. A theory section written in concise and easy to understand language prepares the student for all exercises. Worksheets are given that quiz a student about intervals and chord construction using staff notation. Answers are supplied in the back of the book enabling a student to work without a teacher.

E-Books

The Bruce Arnold series of instructional E-books is for the student who wishes to target specific areas of study that are of particular interest. Many of these books are excerpted from other larger texts. The excerpted source is listed for each book. These books are available on-line at www.muse-eek.com as well as at many e-tailers throughout the internet. These books can also be purchased in the traditional book binding format. (See the ISBN number for proper format)

Chord Velocity: Volume One, Learning to switch between chords quickly
E-book ISBN 1-890944-88-2

The first hurdle a beginning guitarist encounters is difficulty in switching between chords quickly enough to make a chord progression sound like music. This book provides exercises that help a student gradually increase the speed with which they change chords. Special free audio files are also available on the muse-eek.com website to make practice more productive and fun. With a few weeks, remarkable improvement by can be achieved using this method. This book is excerpted from "1st Steps for a Beginning Guitarist Volume One."

Guitar Technique: Volume One, Learning the basics to fast, clean, accurate and fluid performance skills.
E-book ISBN 1-890944-91-2

This book is for both the beginning guitarist or the more experienced guitarist who wishes to improve their technique. All aspects of the physical act of playing the guitar are covered, from how to hold a guitar to the specific way each hand is involved in the playing process. Pictures and videos are provided to help clarify each technique. These pictures and videos are either contained in the book or can be downloaded at www.muse-eek.com This book is excerpted from "1st Steps for a Beginning Guitarist Volume One."

Accompaniment: Volume One, Learning to Play Bass and Chords Simultaneously
E-book ISBN 1-890944-87-4

The techniques found within this book are an excellent resource for creating and understanding how to play bass and chords simultaneously in a jazz or blues style. Special attention is paid to understanding how this technique is created, thereby enabling the student to recreate this style with other pieces of music. This book is excerpted from the book "Guitar Clinic."

Beginning Rhythm Studies: Volume One, Learning the basics of reading rhythm and playing in time.
E-book ISBN 1-890944-89-0

This book covers the basics for anyone wishing to understand or improve their rhythmic abilities. Simple language is used to show the student how to read and play rhythm. Exercises are presented which can accelerate the learning process. Audio examples in the form of midifiles are available on the muse-eek.com website to facilitate learning the correct rhythm in time. This book is excerpted from the book "Rhythm Primer."